D1500188

MICHAEL MYERS

Fly!
An Imprint of Abdo Zoom
abdobooks.com

Kenny Abdo

abdobooks.com

Published by Abdo Zoom, a division of ABDO, P.O. Box 398166, Minneapolis, Minnesota 55439. Copyright © 2020 by Abdo Consulting Group, Inc. International copyrights reserved in all countries. No part of this book may be reproduced in any form without written permission from the publisher. Fly!™ is a trademark and logo of Abdo Zoom.

Printed in the United States of America, North Mankato, Minnesota.
052019
092019

THIS BOOK CONTAINS
RECYCLED MATERIALS

Photo Credits: Alamy, AP Images, Everett Collection, MPTV Images
Production Contributors: Kenny Abdo, Jennie Forsberg, Grace Hansen
Design Contributors: Dorothy Toth, Neil Klinepier

Library of Congress Control Number: 2018963567

Publisher's Cataloging-in-Publication Data

Names: Abdo, Kenny, author.
Title: Michael Myers / by Kenny Abdo.
Description: Minneapolis, Minnesota : Abdo Zoom, 2020 | Series: Hollywood monsters set 2 | Includes online resources and index.
Identifiers: ISBN 9781532127489 (lib. bdg.) | ISBN 9781532128462 (ebook) | ISBN 9781532128950 (Read-to-me ebook)
Subjects: LCSH: Myers, Michael (Fictitious character)--Juvenile literature. | Halloween (Motion picture : 1978)--Juvenile literature. | Horror films--Juvenile literature. | Motion picture characters--Juvenile literature.
Classification: DDC 791.43616--dc23

TABLE OF CONTENTS

MICHAEL MYERS

Halloween is about a man named Michael Myers. On Halloween night, he escapes from a mental **asylum**. He returns to his hometown and terrorizes a group of babysitters.

5

Originally known as "the Shape," Michael Myers has horrified audiences for more than 40 years!

7

ORIGIN

John Carpenter was a fan of the film *Black Christmas*. It is considered one of the first slasher movies. Carpenter wanted to make a similar film. But he wanted it to take place on Halloween, the spookiest night of the year.

Carpenter and his partner, Debra Hill, wrote the **script** in 10 days. Carpenter wrote the action while Hill focused on the **dialog** for the teenage babysitters.

Carpenter wanted his killer to be as unrelatable as possible. The less the audience understood him, the scarier he would be.

HOLLYWOOD

The movie is set in fictional Haddonfield, Illinois. It was actually filmed in Southern California. Fake leaves were spray-painted fall colors and dropped on the streets.

Young, unknown actress Jamie
Lee Curtis was hired to play Laurie
Strode. Her mother, Janet Lee,
starred in *Psycho*, the biggest horror
movie of the time.

The crew bought a cheap mask of *Star Trek's* William Shatner. They spray-painted it white and widened the eye holes. It was creepy because of how emotionless it was.

The movie was a massive hit! It
made more than 70 million dollars
on a $300,000 budget. *Halloween*
is one of the most successful
independent films of all time.

HALLOWEEN II

ALL NEW

A **sequel** quickly followed. By the third film, Carpenter and Hill were done with Myers. Part three came out as a new story and fans were upset. Myers starred in every movie after that.

LEGACY

There are 11 *Halloween* movies. Some are **reboots** of the series, while the rest are **sequels**. A total of 13 actors have played the masked killer!

FAMILY IS FOREVER

A **ROB ZOMBIE** FILM

HALLOWEEN II

DIMENSION FILMS PRESENTS A MALEK AKKAD PRODUCTION A ROB ZOMBIE FILM "HALLOWEEN II" MALCOLM McDOWELL TYLER MANE SHERI MOON ZOMBIE
BRAD DOURIF DANIELLE HARRIS AND SCOUT TAYLOR-COMPTON CASTING MONIKA MIKKELSEN CSA COSTUMES MARY McLEOD MUSIC ROB ZOMBIE SCORE TYLER BATS
EDITED GLENN GARLAND PRODUCTION GARRETH STOVER PHOTOGRAPHY BRANDON TROST EXECUTIVE BOB WEINSTEIN HARVEY WEINSTEIN MATTHEW STEIN ANDY LA MARCA
www.Halloween2-Movie.com PRODUCED MALEK AKKAD ANDY GOULD ROB ZOMBIE WRITTEN DIRECTED ROB ZOMBIE   DIMENSION

AUGUST 28TH EVERYWHERE

19

Myers is featured in novels, comic books, and video games. His white mask is a popular costume on Halloween.

A **sequel** to the 1978 original was released in 2018. A 61-year-old Michael Myers escapes from prison to again hunt Laurie Strode. It is the highest-grossing film in the **franchise**.

GLOSSARY

asylum – an institution that protects and cares for those in need, especially the mentally ill.

dialog – conversation between two or more people in a book or movie.

franchise – a collection of related movies in a series.

reboot – a new start to a movie franchise, recreating plots, characters, and backstory.

script – written text of a movie.

sequel – a movie, or other work that continues the story begun in a preceding one.

ONLINE RESOURCES

Booklinks
NONFICTION NETWORK
FREE! ONLINE NONFICTION RESOURCES

To learn more about
Michael Myers, please visit
abdobooklinks.com or scan
this QR code. These links
are routinely monitored and
updated to provide the most
current information available.

INDEX